WISDOM JIBBER-JABBER

WISDOM JIBBER-JABBER

Graduation Edition

KAREN MURPHY

Copyright © 2022 by Karen Murphy
All rights reserved. Published by Bowl of Stone Fruit Press.
ISBN 978-1-962676-04-5

For Archie

I love you. You're perfect just the way you are, and you don't have to be anything but you.

All your life, people have asked you, "What do you want to be when you grow up?" It's a terrible question, because after those first few years when the answer is clear and obvious to you–astronaut, ballerina, rodeo clown–things start to get a little murky. And as the years go by, maybe the question starts to make you uneasy, because you understand more of the world.

You understand more of what's impossible—let's face it, if you get bitten by a radioactive spider, that's very bad news, not an invitation to hang out with the Avengers—and what's possible but improbable—there are around 450 players in the NBA, out of almost 8 billion people on the planet.

That's not encouraging math.

At the same time, how are you supposed to know what *is* possible? In your experience, you've seen what teachers do, what doctors do, what coaches do. You've seen what your parents' work is like, and maybe their friends' work. Maybe in movies you see examples of architects and ad executives. (And based on my experience, those depictions are wildly inaccurate.)

But how can you have any idea what it's like to be an insurance adjuster or a packaging engineer or a marine electrician?

This question that adults ask the smallest children turns out to be a torture device. Because how can you know? How can you be expected to decide?

Have I worked you into a frenzy of tortured nerves yet? I'm about to soothe them.

I'm going to reveal to you several secrets.

First, the very people who have always asked you what you want to be when you grow up?

They are, for the most part, asking themselves the same question. Unless they've irreversibly retired to the recliner in front of the TV news as a lifestyle, they're still asking themselves what they want to do with their lives.

They ask kids that question because they're looking for ideas.

Second, this question promotes a worldview that has nothing to do with reality.

It suggests that you place yourself on the conveyor belt of career choice A or B or C and, for better or worse, ride it to the end of the line.

I don't know if you've read or studied the poem "The Road Not Taken," by Robert Frost. Super famous poem. Very lovely and evocative.

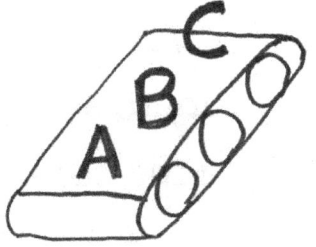

The final lines of the poem read:

> Two roads diverged in a wood, and I—
> I took the one less traveled by,
> And that has made all the difference.

These final lines have been used for more than a century to suggest that you shouldn't take the common path.

Do something different and unexpected, something that calls out to your heart, because you're not like the rest of those slobs who take the well traveled road.

But when you study it in a poetry class, it is revealed that the two roads that diverged in the wood weren't really very different. They seem to be about equally traveled.

And you might learn that Robert Frost was taken aback when his poem was received as a serious comment on how to live life, when he wrote it as a light-hearted take on how which path you choose in the woods might not really be that life-altering.

But I have a different gripe with "The Road Not Taken," because it tells you that there are roads. There are no roads.

Your life takes place on an uncharted landscape. There's rocky terrain, where making your way is rough no matter where you place your foot, and you encounter patches of shale that leave you backsliding no matter how careful you are. There are meadows teeming with wildflowers, each step a springy pleasure. And there are places where there seems to be a hint of a trail, maybe made by goats.

You have no way of knowing what you'll encounter next. Each new part of the world is only revealed when you get to a scenic viewpoint or turn a corner. You can use what you know of what other people have done when *they've* encountered boulders or cliffs. It certainly helps to take sailing lessons and build a boat if you observe that there's a sea between you and where you want to go. But there are no roads. Only what's next and next and next. One choice after another, your life unique and incomparable.

I don't know whether this idea is daunting, terrifying, and overwhelming, or exciting and freeing. It's a lot. Life is—or can be—immense.

So how do you navigate when there are no roads and there is no map? How do you choose a direction or a step?

Here's the joyful answer (and third secret): You are your own compass.

If you can disregard every "should," whether it comes from society at large, your parents, your friends, or your own idea of who you are, your deepest self will tell you where to go. The form of the guidance might come in many different ways.

An irresistible drive to have or do or be. A frisson of eagerness when you think about taking a trip or taking a job. A resistance in your gut to something that looks good on paper. A feeling of standing at the top of a diving board that's too high for comfort–breathless, afraid, but excited, too.

Your job is to listen. Your job is to trust that self and follow.

It's easy to make excuses and to tell yourself little lies, to deny that north is north. But the more you ignore what your compass tells you, the more you will carry yourself into a place that you don't recognize, and the harder it will be to hear that inner voice clearly. It's never too late to listen to yourself and be true to yourself. But the sooner and the more you make a habit of it, the louder and clearer and easier to access that most authentic part of yourself will be.

This doesn't mean that when you listen to and follow that inner compass your life will be easy. It doesn't mean that each stream you cross will have evenly spaced stepping stones. Sometimes, those stones will be slippery. Sometimes you'll have to jump as far as you can to get to the next one. Sometimes, you'll have to backtrack and find a tree branch to fashion a makeshift bridge, or you might have to build a more permanent one.

Sometimes you might slip into the water and be drenched and cold and uncomfortable. Sometimes you might have to do it while you carry something heavy on your back, like two kids and a mortgage.

That brings us to secret four. "It's dangerous to go alone. Take this."

In the game *The Legend of Zelda,* an old man said those words and gave Link a sword. In real life, there are very few situations that are improved by the use of a sword. I mean, machetes are really useful for clearing brush, but swords aren't helpful most of the time. But we have each other.

"It's dangerous to go alone. Take this."

"This" is a piece of useful information or advice from a mentor. It's a gift of time from a bus driver who waits when they see you running to the bus stop, or the empathetic shake of a head from the bystander who saw it all when the bus driver kept going instead.

It's an extra hand when you're trying to build a shed or directions from a stranger when you're lost or the rescue of your dignity by a person who tells you that you have toilet paper on your shoe.

It's the friend who listens. It's the family you choose and build. We are not alone. Other people are there for you, and you're there for them. There's strength in numbers, and we're all in this together.

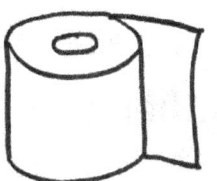

Not everyone will agree with this.

Cynics will tell you, "It's a dog-eat-dog world. Life is a zero-sum game. Get them before they get you."

You'll encounter people who are obstacles, whether it's a petty tyrant at the county permit office or someone who wants the same table you do at a restaurant. And reality is enormous.

For all practical purposes, there are unlimited people in the world who will help you and unlimited people in the world who will oppose you.

Find the ones who will help you. Focus on the ones who will help you. Give as little time and attention to the haters as is reasonably possible. Don't feed the trolls.

Nurture and love other people, and let them love and nurture you, and there won't be time and space in your life to be dragged down by people who don't play fair or who take pleasure from other people's pain.

There may be dogs out there that eat dogs. I haven't met them. In my experience, most dogs are tail-waggers.

Secret five. "The cake is a lie."

Another game reference? That's from *Portal,* which was released in 2007. It's my most current—that is, not current at all—game reference, and is the last meme you'll hear from me today—probably.

Beware the promise of a reward at the end of a journey.

The journey is and must be its own reward, because there is no other promise. It is possible that you'll do everything right and still not get what you'd hoped for. It's possible that you'll get exactly what you'd hoped for and find out its promise was empty. And of course, it's possible that you'll plot a course and follow it, working and adjusting as needed to reach your goal, and it will be everything you imagined and more.

The point is that the end is not the point. The end is only a small part of the overall experience, and if you focus on the end and on the reward, you miss the moments and details that give life its richness and meaning.

Pay attention. Pay attention to the journey, and if you notice ingredients for cake along the way, collect them and bake your own.

And here's the sixth and final secret that I'll share with you today.

I have more secrets—dozens if not hundreds—but psychological research tells us that humans can only remember lists of about five to seven items, and we're at six, so this is where we'll call it quits.

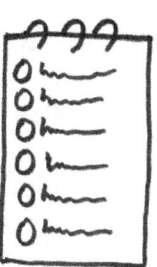

The sixth secret has to do with being a grownup. When are you a grownup?

When do you have the right to call yourself a grownup? When do you have the necessary life experience? The necessary competence? If you don't feel like a grownup today, when will you? When you turn eighteen, if you haven't? Twenty-one? Twenty-five? When you have your first child or buy your first house or get your first raise or are granted your first patent?

18 is a number

There's a simple way to tell when you're a grownup: It's never.

You will never be a grownup. None of us are. You will do amazing things in your life. You'll explore and take on responsibilities and become respected by the community. But it's unlikely that you'll ever feel like a grownup, and you'll certainly never be one.

Because we're all infants. We're all new to the next thing life will bring us or that we'll reach for. We all learn and bumble and fall down and pick ourselves up. We all carry the child we've always been inside us all the time whether we're trying to wrestle them into submission or distract them with shiny objects or we're giving them hugs or taking them on picnics in the park.

If it's what you hope and work for, you'll get better with age, and you'll become more than you are now, but adulthood as a feeling is as much a lie as the cake. You're still just you.

And the exciting part of this is that you're not waiting for your life to start. You're in it now. This is it, the meat of it. Today, and tomorrow, and the next day, and all of the days after that.

The only thing holding you back from doing things is the idea that you're not ready or you have to be a grownup and you're not yet.

You never will be, so why wait?

There will be people who tell you that this isn't true. (Rental car agencies who won't rent to people under 25, I'm looking at you.) That's arbitrary.

Yes, there are people who have more experience than you do. Even when you're the world's preeminent authority in your field, there will be people who have more experience than you do in every other aspect of life.

But you are and always will be the only you. You are the only one in the world who can contribute the uniqueness of your self to the mashup of being that we're all splashing and trudging and dancing around in.

If you don't know how to do something today, use the tools at your disposal—curiosity, other people's knowledge, trial and error, failure and getting up—to move toward knowing how to do it tomorrow or the next day or one of the days after that.

You have everything you need right now to take your next breath, to make your next choice, to take your next step.

And you do that again and again and again and one day someone will surprise you by calling you ma'am or sir (or the more evolved form of elder address of your future).

You'll realize that other people think you're a grownup.

You won't be. But that's our little secret.

So let's review.

One, nobody knows what they want to be when they grow up. Two, life is an uncharted landscape with no roads. Three, you are your own compass. Four, it's dangerous to go alone. Five, the cake is a lie. And six, you'll never be a grownup.

I'm going to give you a bonus seventh secret, because, like you and like life, I'm full of surprises. But this really is going to be the last one, because of that five-to-seven-items thing I mentioned before.

||||| ||

Seven: Kindness will bring you joy and gratitude and fulfillment. Be kind.

Be kind to yourself. You must be kind to yourself. You cannot be kind to anyone else until you are able to be kind to yourself.

If you find that you're unable to be kind to yourself, get therapy. You might have to try a few therapists—or more than a few—or a few different types of therapy before you find one that helps you to be gentle and kind with yourself, but finding tools or people to help you learn to be kind to yourself if you don't already know how is essential.

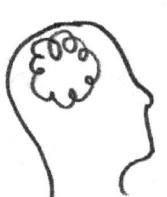

Be kind to other people. Don't let other people's unkindness make you bitter or resentful. If unkindness has a tendency to escalate, so does kindness.

You can't expect that your kindness will always be reciprocated—this isn't a balance sheet. And kindness isn't being a pushover or a doormat. It doesn't mean that you don't stand up for yourself or that you sacrifice your own needs.

It means that you recognize that through the exercise of your agency, you shape the world, even if it's just a little, and you can choose for the world to be a kinder place through your actions.

Seeking to be happy will leave you feeling vaguely unsettled, asking yourself "Is that all there is?"

Striving to be kind, to give a gift of happiness to other people when you can, will make your world one of kindness and happiness, in the way that we sometimes find what we need most when we're looking for something else.

And, bonus, the next time someone asks you what you want to be when you grow up, you'll have an answer.

Tell them "kind."

And then? Tell them "rodeo clown."

Who's gonna stop you?

www.ingramcontent.com/pod-product-compliance
Lightning Source LLC
Chambersburg PA
CBHW031455040426
42444CB00007B/1106